YOUR KNOWLEDGE HAS VALUE

- We will publish your bachelor's and master's thesis, essays and papers

- Your own eBook and book - sold worldwide in all relevant shops

- Earn money with each sale

Upload your text at www.GRIN.com
and publish for free

Bibliographic information published by the German National Library:

The German National Library lists this publication in the National Bibliography; detailed bibliographic data are available on the Internet at http://dnb.dnb.de .

This book is copyright material and must not be copied, reproduced, transferred, distributed, leased, licensed or publicly performed or used in any way except as specifically permitted in writing by the publishers, as allowed under the terms and conditions under which it was purchased or as strictly permitted by applicable copyright law. Any unauthorized distribution or use of this text may be a direct infringement of the author s and publisher s rights and those responsible may be liable in law accordingly.

Imprint:

Copyright © 2017 GRIN Verlag
Print and binding: Books on Demand GmbH, Norderstedt Germany
ISBN: 9783346145277

This book at GRIN:

https://www.grin.com/document/536417

Tung Nguyen

Are Insurance Companies in the UK Avoiding Taxes? Historical Tax Payments over the Last Five Years

GRIN - Your knowledge has value

Since its foundation in 1998, GRIN has specialized in publishing academic texts by students, college teachers and other academics as e-book and printed book. The website www.grin.com is an ideal platform for presenting term papers, final papers, scientific essays, dissertations and specialist books.

Visit us on the internet:

http://www.grin.com/

http://www.facebook.com/grincom

http://www.twitter.com/grin_com

**University of Applied Sciences
Campus Zweibrücken**

Financial Seminar

Subject:
Tax avoidance of insurance companies in the UK

Student:
Tung Nguyen

Table of contents

List of abbreviations 2

List of figures 3

List of tables 4

1 Introduction 5

2 Literature research 6
2.1 Study on tax practice 6
2.2 Tax havens 8

3 Methodology 9
3.1 Tax and profitability ratios 9
3.2 Linear regression analysis 10
3.3 Limitations 10

4 Results and discussion 11
4.1 Subsidiaries in tax havens 11
4.2 Tax and profitability ratios analysis 11
4.3 Linear regression analysis 14

5 Conclusion 16

6 References 17

Appendix 19

List of abbreviations

TOR	Tax on Return
ROS	Return on Sales
ROAE	Return on Average Equity
SD	Standard Deviation
m	million
bn	billion

List of figures

Fig. 1: Return on Sales ratio of 10 companies.   13

Fig. 2: Return on Average Equity ratio of 10 companies.   14

List of tables

Table 1 & 2. Linear regression analysis TOR and ROS   14

Table 3 & 4. Linear regression analysis TOR and ROAE   15

1 Introduction

In the current age of expanding globalisation and increasing international integration, large corporations and individuals may hold stream of incomes and expenses in multiple countries with different legislation all around the globe. As a result, the matter of tax practices become more and more complicated. In the case of insurance companies, the issue becomes even more complicated due to the nature and characteristics of the streams of income and expense in this industry. In spite of advanced complicated tax legislation in developed nations and reports by specialists, the concern for whether companies such as insurance companies are avoiding taxes or not is growing. (Sikka, 2016) criticise PwC report on taxes by banks and insurance companies. The report indicate that the financial sector paid about £28.8bn of corporate tax, national insurance and business rates. However, Sikka argued that these figures cannot be verified from the companies' reports as there is little information about the taxes they paid in the UK or elsewhere.

The insurance industry in the UK is the fourth largest in the World and the largest in the Euro with about one-fourth of insurance premium in the whole Euro area generated in the country. The industry, in 2014, contribute to around £12bn in taxes to the UK government (ABI, 2015). In this analysis, historical tax payment in the last five years (from 2011 to 2015) of 10 insurance companies in the UK would be investigated and analyses thoroughly to answer this question. These companies are among the top 14 insurance companies in the UK in term of assets (Relbanks, 2017) (Appendix 1).

2 Literature research

2.1 Study on tax practice

According to Institute of Business Ethics (2013), companies minimise their tax payment by "tax planning", making the most of legal tools including all allowances, deductions, rebates, exemption, etc. These are considered as compliant behaviour. Companies can engage with tax avoidance which refers to bending the rule of the tax system, although legitimate, to obtain tax result not intended by the government. Company directors often argue that they are responsible for maximising shareholder's value, including keeping tax cost as low as possible under legislation. In a study of tax planning effects, (Ifada & Wulandari (2015) stated earning management can take advantage of tax rate by shifting profit before changes in corporate tax rates to a year after the change takes place. Under accounting rule, this follows the principal of accrual basis (revenues are reported in income statement when they are earned, whereas under cash basis, revenues are reported when cash is received).

Although tax avoidance is different from tax evasion, which is illegally reducing tax liabilities by falsely reporting income or expenditure (Hall, 2015), it is considered as unethical. Paying a fair amount of taxes is sociable responsibilities of companies, as it provided fund for public service such as education, healthcare and public infrastructure. Avoiding taxes can detriment company's image and sociality's trust in them. Her majesty's Revenue and Customs (2016) estimated that there was £3.7bn of corporate tax gap for 2014-2015 period (£3.3 billion in 2013-2014), which is the different between the amount should be collected, in theory, by HMRC and the actual collected amount. This represents 10% of the overall tax gap. Companies such as Google, Starbucks and Amazon faced negative criticism for tax avoidance and lack of transparency (Barford & Holt, 2013). In 2011, Google's UK unit made a profit of £395m but pay only £6 million of tax. Starbucks paid almost no corporation tax while making £400m of profit. Amazon paid £1.8m over £3.35bn of return. Despite these small tax payment on return, all of these companies business activities are legal.

Which income of a company is taxable? According to Sayari & Muğan (2014), financial income (book income) is income reported in financial statement for the use by shareholders, investors or business to make appropriate financial judgements. On the other hand, taxable income reporting is prepared for tax authorities to calculate a company's tax liabilities. Dierent objective s give lead to dierent principles and rules. Some revenues and expenses are included in financial income but not in taxable income and vice versa. For instant, municipal bond interest is included in financial income but excluded in tax income. Timing of recognition of incomes and expenses also cause the difference.

The difference between the two income reports is often called the book-tax gap. Tran (2015) stated the book-tap gap exists not only because of the different reporting rule, but also because companies (or their managers) have various incentives to adjust financial income and taxable income in different directions. Lack of information transparency between managers and outside stakeholders allows managers to take advantage of private information when they chose accounting procedures in order to obtain some private gains or the shareholders. There is a debates in the US on whether public companies should be required to reveal taxable income report (Tran, 2015).

According to Mill and Plesko (2003, cited by Sayari and Muğan, 2014), the first reason for book-tax gaps to exist is when companies have foreign or domestic subsidiaries with less than 100% ownership. If a company own more than 50% but less than 100% of shares of a subsidiary, it should subtract a portion of the subsidiary's income from its net income and put that amount in the minority shareholder interest. If the ownership is between 20% and 50%, the company should include its interest of the subsidiary income as "net equity of unconsolidated subsidiaries". Finally, if the company owns less than 20% of shares, it should only include dividends of the subsidiary in financial income. The second reason is that financial accounting prevents companies from overstating income, while taxation rules prevents companies from understating income. Companies would try to increase reported book income to boost their market value while lower reported taxable income to pay less tax.

Difference of financial income reported to shareholders and income reported to tax authority is a potential evidence of growing tax avoidance activity (Green and Plesko, 2016).

2.2 Tax havens

Companies can reduce tax liabilities by establishing subsidiaries in tax havens, where there is low or even zero tax rates. Tax havens also provide secrecy for transactions as they share no financial information with foreign tax authorities. The subsidiaries in tax havens charge a fee to the parent companies; therefore, profits of these parent companies are transferred away from higher-tax countries into tax havens. A report by Actionaid (2013) found that among the FTSE 100 companies, 98 of them use tax havens, locating 38% (8.492) of their subsidiaries. In fact, the number of companies registered by the FTSE 100 in China (551) is even fewer than on the tiny island of Jersey (623).

The European Union has published a list of tax havens to restrict the tax avoidance activities (EU Business, 2015). The full list is: Andorra, Liechtenstein, Guernsey, Monaco, Mauritius, Liberia, Seychelles, Brunei, Hong Kong, Maldives, Cook Islands, Nauru, Niue, Marshall Islands, Vanuatu, Anguilla, Antigua and Barbuda, Bahamas, Barbados, Belize, Bermuda, British Virgin Islands, Cayman Islands, Grenada, Montserrat, Panama, St Vincent and the Grenadines, St Kitts and Nevis, Turks and Caicos, US Virgin Islands.

According to PwC's worldwide tax summaries (2015), in Jersey the 10% tax rate applies to financial services companies. Companies in Guernsey pay 0% corporate tax rate. Bermuda has no taxes on profits, income, dividends, or capital gains, as well as no limit on the accumulation of profit, and has no requirement to distribute dividends. Cayman Islands does not tax foreign companies on income earned outside of the islands. In Hong Kong, capital gains and dividends are not subjected to taxation. Income gained abroad is also not taxed. Additionally, companies in Hong Kong are not required to prepare financial statements with any authority. This is just to name a few.

Based on the EU's list, the analysis examines whether the 10 chosen insurance companies have subsidiaries in these tax havens, as well as the percentage in relation with total number of subsidiaries.

3 Methodology
3.1 Tax and profitability ratios

This report analyses the relation between the tax on return ratio with indicators of company's profitability, including Return on Sales (ROS), Return on Average Equity (ROAE).

The following formulas were used:

Tax on return: $\text{TOR} = \dfrac{\text{Tax}}{\text{Return before tax}}$

Return on Sales: $\text{ROS} = \dfrac{\text{Return before tax}}{\text{Gross premium}}$

Return on Average Equity:

$\text{ROAE} = \dfrac{\text{Return before tax}}{(\text{Equity at the end of the year} + \text{Equity at the beginning of the year})/2}$

Return on Equity ratio inform how much profit a company makes with the money shareholders have invested. Return On Average Equity ratio replaces equity by average equity, which is the mean of equity at the end and the beginning of the fiscal year.

The average ROS ratio and average ROE ratio of the whole period are calculated by taking the mean of ratios of each year. Whereas the TOR ratio of the whole period is calculated by taking accumulated tax paid divided by accumulated return before tax.

The analysis looked at annual reports of these companies from 2011 to 2015. The figures were taken from their consolidated financial statement; therefore, they present the whole group companies finance including their subsidiaries.

Data values which significantly differ from others in a data set are considered outliers. In this analysis, outliers are recognised by quartile method. Data higher than upper bound (*third quartile + 1.5 x interquartile*) or lower than lower bound (*first quartile – 1.5 x interquartile*) are considered outliers. The first quartile is the point that 25% of the data is smaller and the third quartile is the point that 25% of the data is larger. Interquartile is the result of subtracting the first quartile from the third quartile.

3.2 Linear regression analysis

Linear regression analysis is used to measure relationships between two variables and predict one dependant variable from another independent variable (Field 2005). Regression analysis predicts an outcome variable from one or several predictor variable(s). In regression, the model to predict data is linear, which has the following equation:

$$Y_i = (\beta_0 + \beta_1 X_i) + \varepsilon_i$$

with Y_i is the outcome, X_i is the predictor variable, β_0 and β_1 are regression coefficient and ε_i is the difference between predicted and actually obtained score (Field, 2009). A positive or negative β_1 indicates a positive or negative relationship between Y_i and X_i. In this research, this analysis helps examine the relationship TOR - ROS and TOR - ROAE.

The ANOVA analysis (analysis of variance) helps indicate whether the model results are significantly good at predicting the outcome variable. For example, a significant of 0.001 indicates there is 0.1% chance that the F-ratio $\left(F = \dfrac{the\ mean\ squares\ for\ the\ model}{the\ residual\ mean\ squares}\right)$ would happen if there is a null hypothesis. In this case, the regression model can predict the outcome variable (Field, 2009).

3.3 Limitations

The analysis has several limitations. All of the information is only gathered from the companies' annual reports. However, these annual reports do not include taxable income; therefore, it is not possible to know how the companies' tax liabilities are calculated. Financial statements do not present other expenses of the companies clearly, which could be a tool to reduce tax liabilities. Income and tax payment of subsidiaries are not included, especially those located in tax havens. Sample is in short time span and may not present the whole industry.

4 Results and discussion

4.1 Subsidiaries in tax havens

From the observation of the 10 chosen companies' 2015 annual reports, a significant number of these companies' subsidiaries have been spotted locating in well-known tax havens. These tax havens include the British overseas territories and islands (Bermuda, Cayman Islands, The Isle of Man, Jersey and Guernsey), Hong Kong, Luxembourg, Ireland, Delaware (USA's state) and other countries in Africa. Aviva has the highest number of subsidiaries in tax havens (166), followed by Old Mutual (107) and Prudential plc (95). RSA Insurance Group (31) has the highest proportion of subsidiaries in tax havens. In contrast, Direct Line, Amlin plc and NFU Mutual have the least numbers (1, 2 and 6). Legal & General and Phoenix Holdings have slightly equal numbers and proportion (12 and 14). Number of Standard Life's subsidiaries was not possible to be counted as the company has security protection in their annual reports. As a whole, 13.21% of the nine companies' subsidiaries located in tax havens. (Appendix 1)

4.2 Tax and profitability ratios analysis

Regarding the percentage of tax paid in proportion with return before tax, the rate vary greatly from -2350% to 303.77%. Aside from the outliers of -2350%,

-63.82%, -38.52%, -23.98, -22.86 182.11% and 303.77% the range of percentage of tax paid vary from -8.95% to 44.05%. (Appendix 3)

According to the Trading Economics, (2016), the corporate tax rate in the UK was 26% in 2011, 24% in 2012, 23% in 2013, 21% in 2014 and 20% in 2015. The average rate from 2011 to 2015 is 22.8%, which is exceed by 6 companies: Legal and General (26.51%), Aviva plc (36.48%), Standard Life (37.04%), Old Mutual (31.6), RSA Insurance Group (58.69%) and Direct Line (24.03%). Phoenix Group Holdings has TOR ratio of 4% of the whole period, followed by Amlin plc (13.89%), NFU Mutual (15.23%) and Prudential plc (18.82%), which are all lower than the average corporate tax rate. (Appendix 3)

Moreover, looking at individual companies, some hold suspicious tax practice behaviour. For example, Phoenix Group Holdings possess the most volatile TOR ratio varying from -2350% to 32.5% in 2011 and 2014 respectively. Except 2014, TOR ratios in other years of Phoenix Group Holdings were below the corporate tax rate in the UK. From 2011 to 2015, the company made totally £225.2m of profit while paid totally £9m of tax, hence only 4% TOR ratio of the period. (Appendix 3)

Amlin plc and Prudential plc had TOR ratio lower than the corporate tax rate in the UK during the whole period. NFU Mutual, aside from 2011, had 4 year of tax underpaid. On the other hand, Direct Line and Legal % General seem to pay somewhat a fair amount of tax. Old Mutual (31.60%), Aviva plc (36.48%), Standard Life (37.04%) and RSA Insurance Group paid significantly higher than the country's tax rate, especially RSA Insurance Group (58.69%) made the highest percentage. (Appendix 3)

Looking at standard deviation, Phoenix Group Holdings, RSA Insurance Group and Aviva plc are companies which have the most volatile TOR ratio. Amlin plc, without an abnormally low ratio in 2011, has a stable TOR trend from 2012 to 2015 (SD=1.27%). NFU Mutual, Legal & General, Standard Life and Old Mutual have a moderate level of fluctuation (SD=12.71%, SD=10.91%, SD=6.04% and SD=5.47%). Prudential plc and Direct Line have the lowest level of fluctuation during the whole period (SD=2.9%). (Appendix 3)

Old Mutual, NFU Mutual and Phoenix Group Holdings were the most efficiency in term of profitability on sales, with average ROS ratio of 37.11%, 30.39% and 19.90% respectively. (Figure 1)

NFU Mutual and Phoenix Group Holding had abnormally high ROS ratio of 60.17% and 47.4%, increased 190% and 332% compared to previous year respectively. Additionally, these companies have the most volatile ROS ratio (SD= 23.96% and SD=17.37%). These are suspicious behaviours considering results from TOR analysis. Phoenix Group Holdings is the company which pay the least tax in proportion with return. In contrast to a sharp rise in profit efficiency, NFU Mutual had similar rate of TOR in 2012 (17.7%) and 2013 (18.1%). Amlin plc, which had an abnormal increase in ROS from 2011 to 2012, also paid very low tax rate (13.89%), just behind Phoenix Group Holding. (Figure 1)

RSA Insurance Group and Aviva plc had the lowest average ROS ratios (2.3% and 5.2%). This seems reasonable as those company paid a large amount of tax in relation with return (36.48% and 58.69%). (Figure 1)

Old Mutual seems to be less suspicious as the company have less fluctuate ROS ratios while paying high tax ratio (31.60%). Legal & General, Direct Line, Prudential plc and Standard Life stand in the middle. These companies also have less volatile ROS ratio (SD= 4.36%, SD=4.36%, SD=1.53% and SD=9.06%) while paying a somewhat fair tax rate. (Figure 1 and Appendix 3)

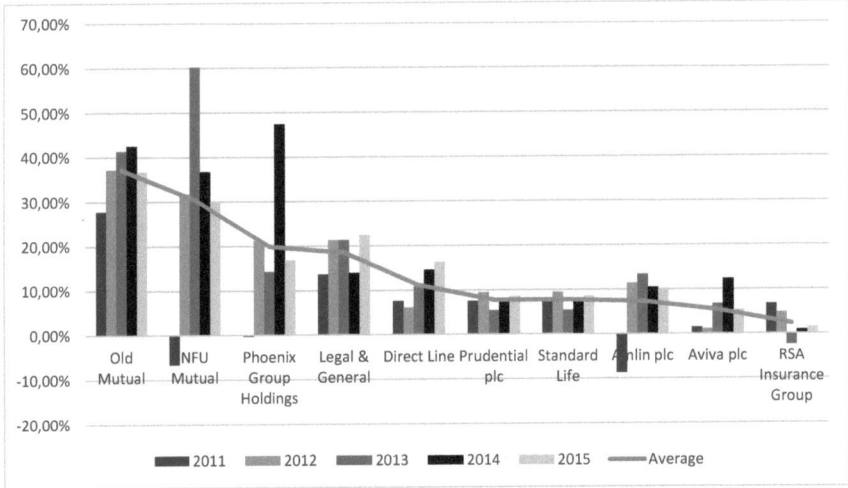

Figure 1. Return on Sales ratio of 10 companies.

Companies, those made moderate return on sales, turn out to have better and less volatile return on average equity ratio, including Prudential plc (23.32%, SD=4.43%), Legal & General (21.33%, SD=3.43%), Standard Life (15.7%, SD=3.72%), Old Mutual (13.51%, SD=2.78%) and Direct Life (13.37%, SD=4.78%). Despite high ROS ratio, NFU Mutual and Phoenix Group Holdings have low and volatile ROAE ratio (9.55%, SD=8.34% and 8.27%, SD=6.44%). Amlin plc had high ROAE from 2012 to 2015 but its average was significantly reduced because of a big loss in 2011. It also had the most unstable ROAE (SD=13.3%). (Figure 2)

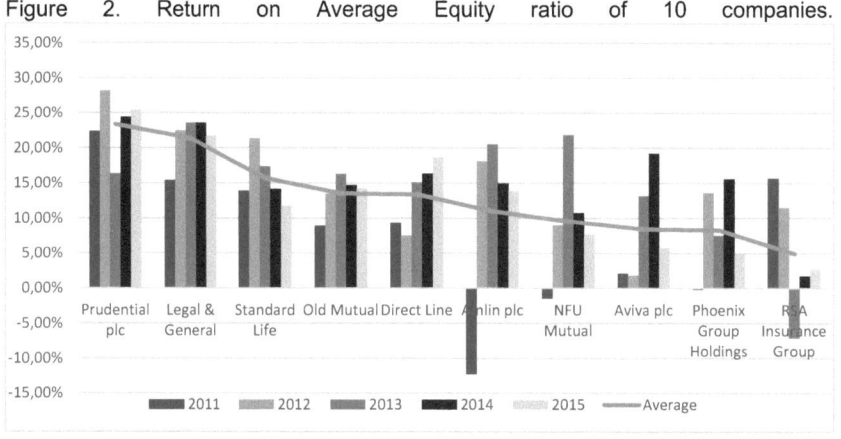

Figure 2. Return on Average Equity ratio of 10 companies.

4.3 Linear regression analysis

After using linear regression analysis in SPSS, the results (table 1 and 3) show that the regression models which demonstrate the relations between TOR and ROS, TOR and ROAE do not demonstrate the necessary level of significant (Sig.=0.490 > 0.05 and Sig.=0.351 > 0.05). Therefore, tax on returns ratio is not predicted by return on sales and return on average equity. The coefficient values are positive (0.130 and 0.119) which show that if ROS and ROAE increase so TOR will increase.

ANOVA[a]

Model		Sum of Squares	df	Mean Square	F	Sig.
1	Regression	96334.046	1	96334.046	.830	.367[b]
	Residual	5568726.323	48	116015.132		
	Total	5665060.368	49			

a. Dependent Variable: TOR b. Predictors: (Constant), ROS

Coefficients[a]

Model		Unstandardized Coefficients		Standardized Coefficients	t	Sig.
		B	Std. Error	Beta		
1	(Constant)	-65.092	69.156		-.941	.351
	ROS	3.066	3.364	.130	.911	.367

a. Dependent Variable: TOR

Table 1 & 2. Linear regression analysis TOR and ROS

NOVA[a]

Model		Sum of Squares	df	Mean Square	F	Sig.
1	Regression	79785.413	1	79785.413	.686	.412[b]
	Residual	5585274.955	48	116359.895		
	Total	5665060.368	49			

a. Dependent Variable: TOR
b. Predictors: (Constant), ROAE

Coefficients[a]

Model		Unstandardized Coefficients		Standardized Coefficients	t	Sig.
		B	Std. Error	Beta		
1	(Constant)	-82.713	89.922		-.920	.362
	ROAE	5.192	6.271	.119	.828	.412

a. Dependent Variable: TOR

Table 3 & 4. Linear regression analysis TOR and ROAE

5 Conclusion

In conclusion, there may need to be more investigation into the situation to ascertain whether companies in insurance industry are avoiding taxes or not. However, from this little investigation, it is undouble that these companies in this industry have suspicious tax practice behaviour. Number of their subsidiaries located in tax havens are significantly high. TOR ratio of some companies are lower than corporate tax rate and/or fluctuate. Profit efficiency in term of return and equity of some companies are abnormally high and could increase two to three times while paying the same tax rate. From the linear analysis result it can be concluded that ROS and ROAE have no significant effect on TOR. Concerning limitation of the analysis, further study is suggested to gather a larger sample of the entire industry in a wider time span.

6 References

ABI. (2015). UK Insurance Key Facts 2016. Retrieved from https://www.abi.org.uk/~/media/files/documents/publications/public/2015/statistics/key%20facts%202015.pdf

Actionaid. (2013). How Tax Havens Plunder the Poor. Retrieved from http://www.gfintegrity.org/wp-content/uploads/2014/05/ActionAid-Tax-Havens-May-2013.pdf

Barford, V & Holt, G. (2013). Google, Amazon, Starbucks: The rise of 'tax shaming'. Retrieved from http://www.bbc.com/news/magazine-20560359

Danielle H. Green and George A. Plesko. (2016). THE RELATION BETWEEN BOOK AND TAXABLE INCOME SINCE THE INTRODUCTION OF THE SCHEDULE M~3. *National Tax Journal,* ,763-784, 69(4), 763–784.

EU Business. (2015). EU releases world tax havens blacklist. Retrieved from http://www.eubusiness.com/news-eu/economy-politics.120n

Field, A. (2009). *DISCOVERING STATISTICS USING SpSS* (3rd ed.). London: SAGE Publications Ltd. Retrieved from http://www.soc.univ.kiev.ua/sites/default/files/library/elopen/andy-field-discovering-statistics-using-spss-third-edition-20091.pdf

Hall, K. S. (2015). The Ethics of Tax Avoidance and Tax Evasion. Retrieved from http://www.neumann.edu/about/publications/NeumannBusinessReview/journal/Review2015/Hall.pdf

Her majesty's Revenue and Customs. (2016). Measuring tax gaps 2016 edition: Tax gap estimates for 2014-15. Retrieved from https://www.gov.uk/government/uploads/system/uploads/attachment_data/file/561312/HMRC-measuring-tax-gaps-2016.pdf

IBE. (2013). Tax Avoidance as an Ethical Issues for Business. *Business Ethics Briefing, 31*. Retrieved from https://www.ibe.org.uk/userassets/briefings/ibe_briefing_31_tax_avoidance_as_an_ethical_issue_for_business.pdf

Ifada, L. M., & Wulandari, N. (2015). The effect of deferred tax and tax planning toward earnings management practice: an empirical study on non-manufacturing companies listed in indonesia stock exchange in the period of 2008-2012. *Interna-*

tional Journal of Organizational Innovation, 8(1), 155–170.

PwC. (2015). Worldwide Tax Summaries: Corporate Taxes 2015/16. Retrieved from https://www.pwc.com/gx/en/tax/corporate-tax/worldwide-tax-summaries/assets/pwc-worldwide-tax-summaries-corporate-2015-16.pdf

Relbanks. (2017). http://www.relbanks.com/top-insurance-companies/uk. Retrieved from http://www.relbanks.com/top-insurance-companies/uk

Sayari, N., & Can Muğan, F. N. (2014). Comparison of book income and taxable income in terms of value relevance of earnings. *World Of Accounting Science*, 16(1), 1–20.

Sikka, P. (2016). Heard the latest Christmas story? It's about how UK banks pay all their taxes. Retrieved from https://www.theguardian.com/commentisfree/2016/dec/08/tax-avoidance-banks-city-london-corporation

Trading Economics. (2016). United Kingdom Corporate Tax Rate. Retrieved from http://www.tradingeconomics.com/united-kingdom/corporate-tax-rate

Tran, A. (2015). Can taxable income be estimated from financial reports of listed companies in Australia? *Australian Tax Forum*, 30, 569–594. Retrieved from https://papers.ssrn.com/sol3/papers.cfm?abstract_id=2666308

Appendix

Appendix 1. List of top 14 insurance companies

Rank	Insurance company	Total Assets (GBP, b)	Balance sheet
1	Legal & General	395.312	30/06/2015
2	Aviva plc	387.874	31/12/2015
3	Prudential plc	386.985	31/12/2015
4	Standard Life	176.722	31/12/2015
5	Old Mutual	133.548	31/12/2015
6	Friends Life Group *	109.521	31/12/2014
7	Phoenix Group Holdings	67.270	30/06/2015
8	AEGON UK	64.368	30/06/2015
9	RSA Insurance Group	20.611	31/12/2015
10	NFU Mutual	15.486	31/12/2014
11	Liverpool Victoria (LV=)	14.539	31/12/2015
12	AIG Europe Limited	13.904	31/12/2014
13	Direct Line Insurance Group	9.957	31/12/2015
14	Amlin plc **	7.008	31/12/2015

* Friends Life Group (formerly Resolution Ltd) was acquired by Aviva in April 2015.
** Amlin was acquired by Mitsui Sumitomo Insurance Group in February 2016.

Appendix 2. Tax havens

Company	Tax havens used	Number of subsidiaries in tax havens	Number of subsidiaries	Percentage
RSA Insurance Group	Guernsey, Jersey, Ireland, Isle of Man, Luxembourg	31	92	33.70%
Prudential plc	Bermuda, Hong Kong, Ireland, Jersey, Cayman Islands, Isle of Man, Guernsey, Luxem-	95	462	20.56%

	bourg			
NFU Mutual	Guernsey, Jersey	6	41	14.63%
Aviva plc	Bermuda, Hong Kong, Ireland, Jersey, Barbados	166	1313	12.64%
Old Mutual	Bermuda, Hong Kong, Ireland, Jersey, Guernsey, Cayman Islands, Panama, Delaware, Isle of Man	107	913	11.72%
Legal & General	Bermuda, Hong Kong, Ireland, Jersey	12	159	7.55%
Phoenix Group Holdings	Bermuda, Ireland, Jersey, Guernsey, Cayman Islands	14	223	6.28%
Direct Line	Jersey	1	25	4.00%
Amlin plc	Bermuda, Ireland	2	57	3.51%
Standard Life	Luxembourg, Jersey, Cayman Islands, Bahamas, Mauritius, Guernsey	Not available		
Total		434	3285	13.21%

Appendix 3.

Company	Average ROS	Average ROE	TOR (whole period)
Phoenix Group Holdings	17.88%	8.42%	4.00%
Amlin plc	7.60%	11.10%	13.89%
NFU Mutual	30.51%	8.40%	15.23%
Prudential plc	7.80%	23.44%	18.82%
Direct Line	10.58%	12.90%	24.03%
Legal & General	18.00%	21.47%	26.51%
Old Mutual	37.03%	13.34%	31.60%
Aviva plc	5.17%	7.73%	36.48%
Standard Life	21.74%	15.69%	37.04%
RSA Insurance Group	2.30%	5.25%	58.69%

Appendix 4

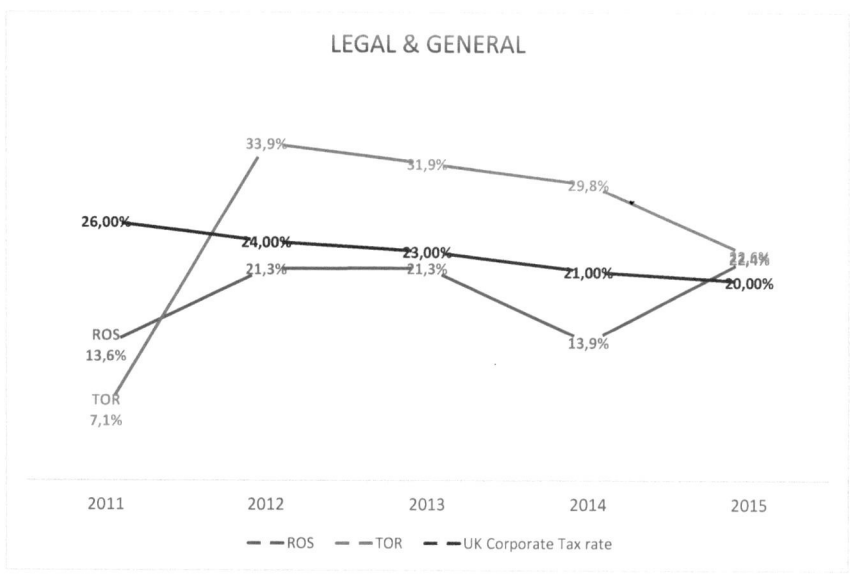

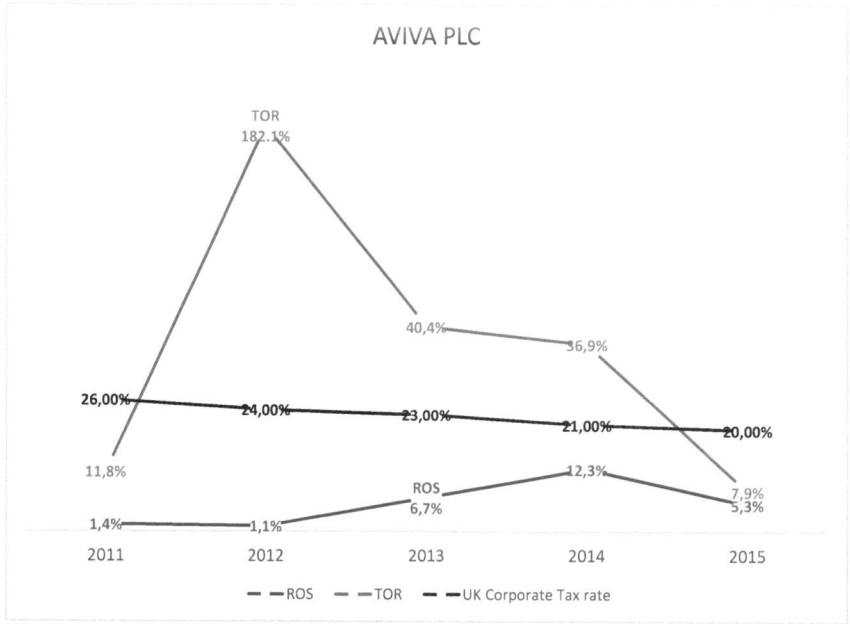

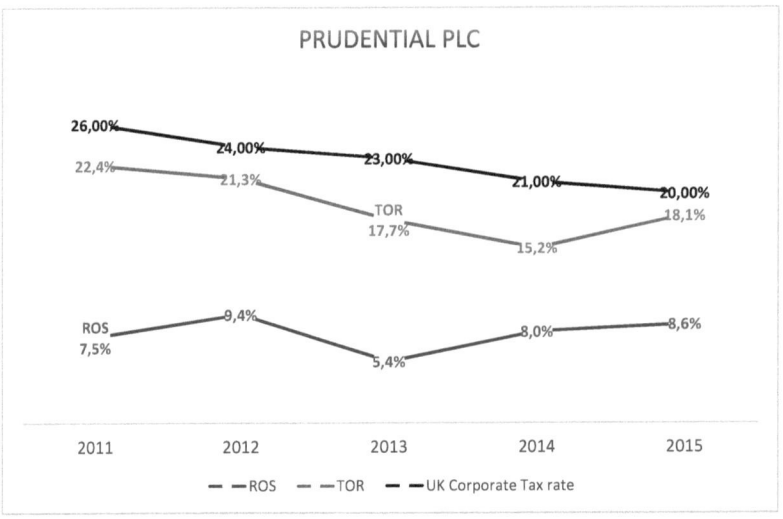

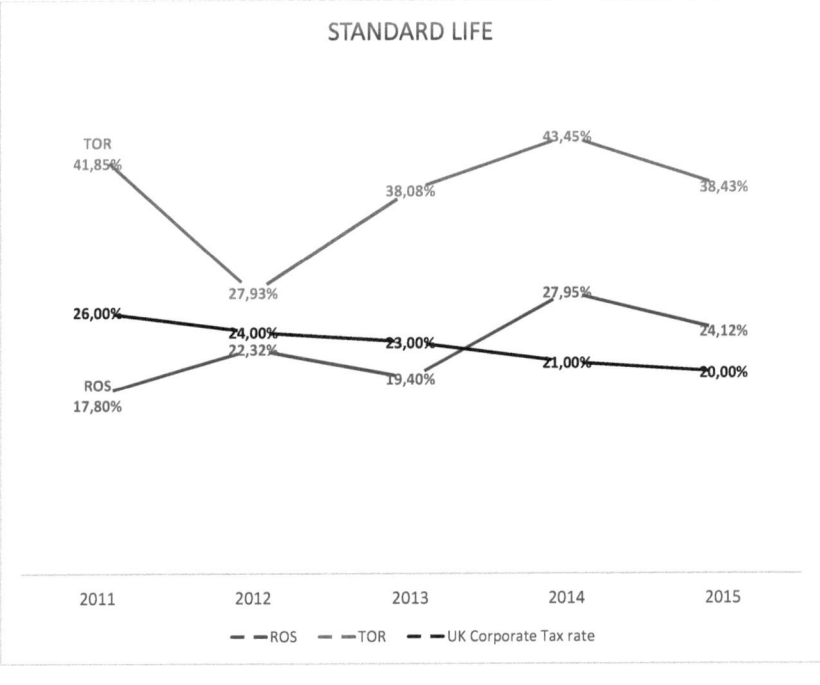

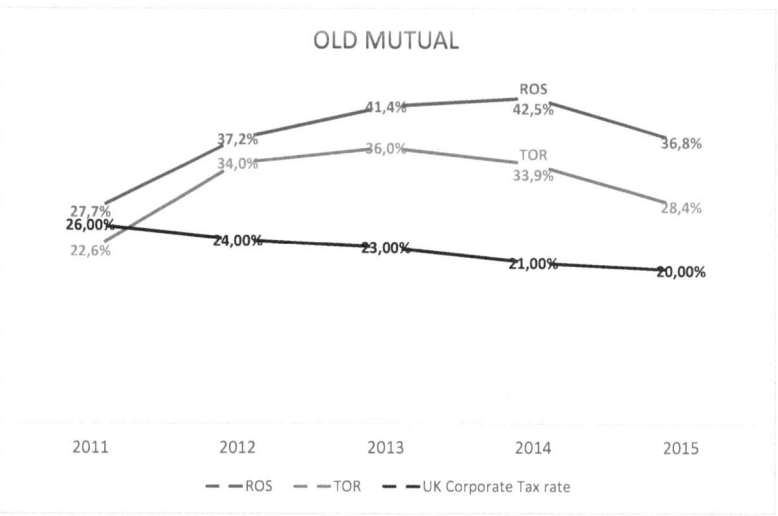

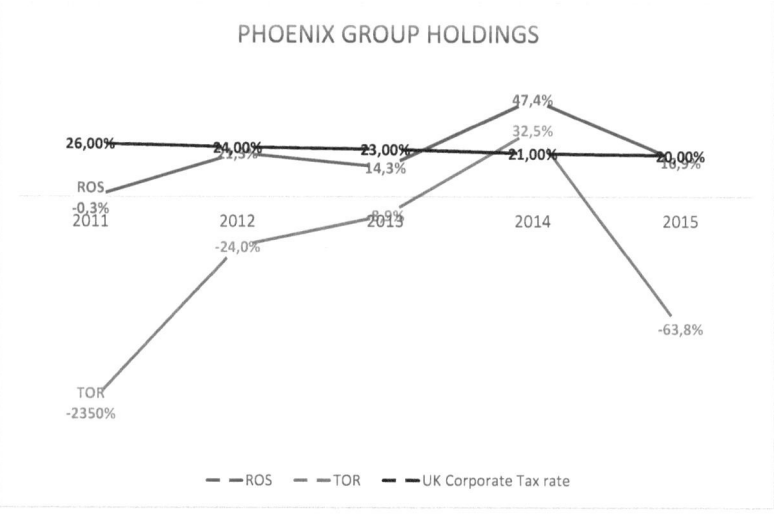

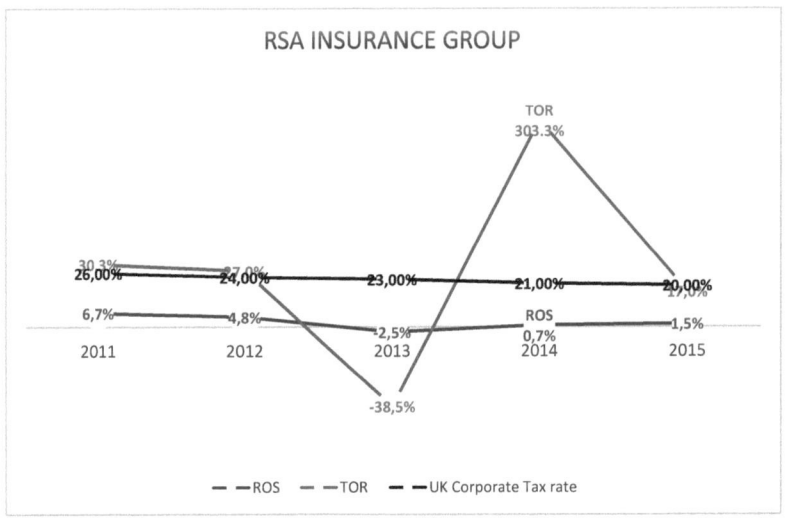

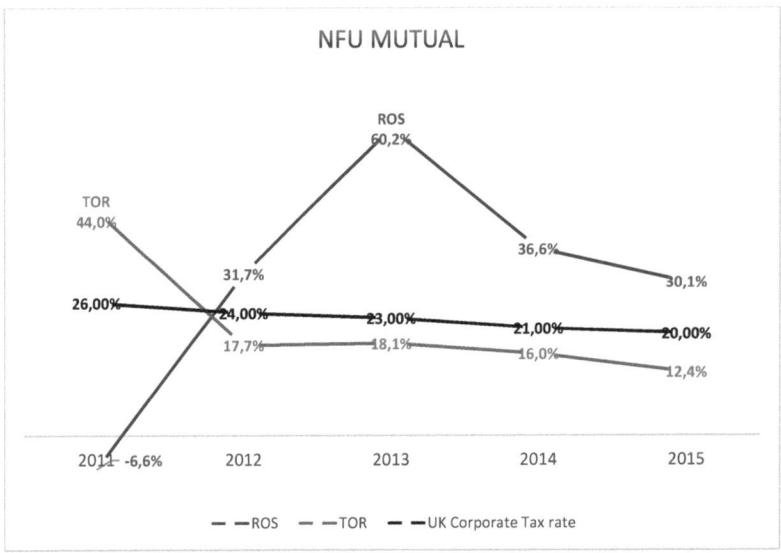

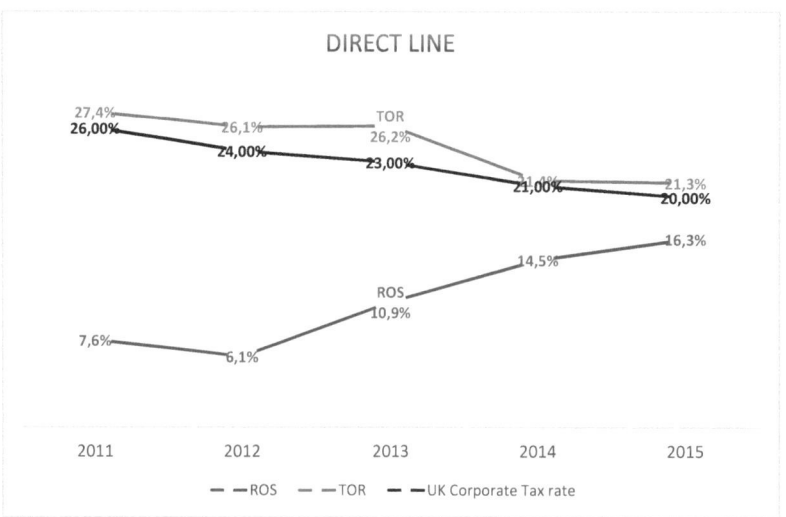

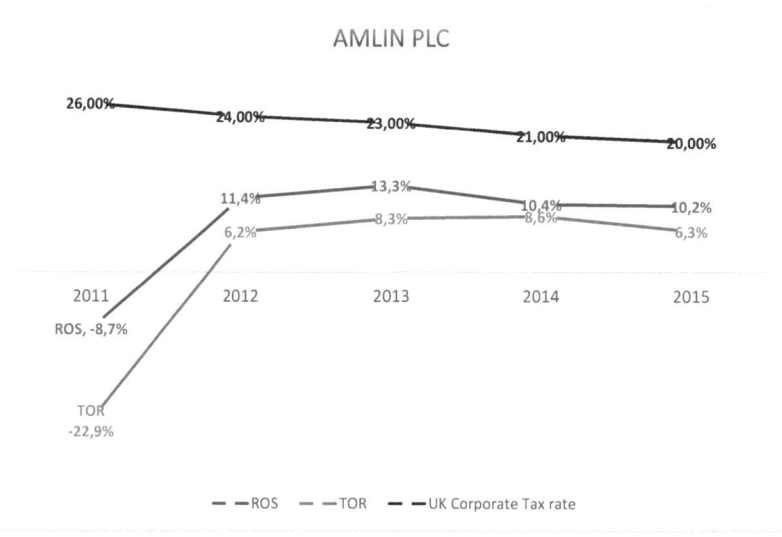

Appendix 5. Tax on return percentage

Company	2011	2012	2013	2014	2015	Standard Deviation
Phoenix Group Holdings	*-2350%*	*-23.98%*	-8.95%	32.47%	*-63.82%*	1044.34%
RSA Insurance Group	30.34%	27.01%	*-38.52%*	*303.77%*	16.98%	134.76%
Aviva plc	11.80%	*182.11%*	40.35%	36.91%	7.94%	72.07%
Amlin plc	*-22.86%*	6.21%	8.29%	8.62%	6.34%	13.56%
NFU Mutual	44.05%	17.71%	18.06%	16.02%	12.44%	12.71%
Legal & General	7.07%	33.89%	31.86%	29.79%	22.63%	10.91%
Standard Life	41.85%	27.93%	38.08%	43.45%	38.43%	6.04%
Old Mutual	22.64%	34.01%	36.03%	33.87%	28.35%	5.47%
Prudential plc	22.43%	21.26%	17.68%	15.23%	18.07%	2.90%
Direct Line	27.41%	26.10%	26.18%	21.44%	21.26%	2.90%
Standard Deviation (all)	340.02%					

Appendix 6. Tax on return percentage (without outliers)

Companies	2011	2012	2013	2014	2015	Standard Deviation
Phoenix Group Holdings	-	-	-8.95%	32.47%	-	29.29%
Aviva plc	11.80%	-	40.35%	36.91%	7.94%	16.74%
NFU Mutual	44.05%	17.71%	18.06%	16.02%	12.44%	12.71%

Legal & General	7.07%	33.89%	31.86%	29.79%	22.63%	10.91%
RSA Insurance Group	30.34%	27.01%	-	-	16.98%	6.95%
Standard Life	41.85%	27.93%	38.08%	43.45%	38.43%	6.04%
Old Mutual	22.64%	34.01%	36.03%	33.87%	28.35%	5.47%
Prudential plc	22.43%	21.26%	17.68%	15.23%	18.07%	2.90%
Direct Line	27.41%	26.10%	26.18%	21.44%	21.26%	2.90%
Amlin plc	-	6.21%	8.29%	8.62%	6.34%	1.27%
Standard Deviation (all)	11.99%					

YOUR KNOWLEDGE HAS VALUE

- We will publish your bachelor's and master's thesis, essays and papers

- Your own eBook and book - sold worldwide in all relevant shops

- Earn money with each sale

Upload your text at www.GRIN.com
and publish for free